Happy for Life: Ten Key Strategies

WILL ROSS

Copyright © 2014 Will Ross

All rights reserved.

DEDICATION

To Debbie Joffe Ellis

CONTENTS

	Introduction	1
1	Choose the direction of your life	3
2	Separate unhelpful feelings from helpful feelings	5
3	Recognize the three major demands	8
4	Replace your demands with preferences	10
5	Use the ABC model	12
6	Create a rational coping statement	15
7	Practice using REBT regularly	17
8	Be ready when you revert back to old habits	19
9	Reach out of your comfort zone	21
10	Choose to be rational	23
	About the author	25
	Author's note	26

INTRODUCTION

This is your life. What do you think of it so far? Are you having a good time? Or does your life seem like a struggle — one giant pain in the butt?

If you're like most people, you've probably had a bit of both — times you enjoy and times you don't enjoy.

The purpose of this booklet is to show you how to enjoy more of your life and have fewer moments of despair. You'll learn ten techniques and strategies to help you lead an ethical, rewarding, and joyful life — a life guided by compassion and reason.

I didn't develop these techniques and strategies. They were developed by Dr Albert Ellis, an American psychologist who, in 1955, created the very first cognitive behavior therapy. Dr Ellis called his therapy *Rational Emotive Behavior Therapy* (REBT). Shortly before his death, in 2007, Dr Ellis asked me to continue his work by teaching REBT to others.

Since 1955, psychologists all over the world have been teaching these methods to their clients to help them deal with a comprehensive range of common human problems and areas of personal growth, including:

- Worry, fear, anxiety, and phobias.
- Guilt, shame, and embarrassment.
- Depression.
- Anger, violence, and rage.
- Relationship issues.
- Sexual problems.
- Addictions.
- Parenting issues, as well as childhood and adolescent problems.
- Weight control.
- Coping with a fatal disease and other health issues.
- Procrastination, self-motivation, and self-discipline.
- Post-traumatic stress disorder (PTSD).

The ten techniques and strategies you'll learn in this book will help you feel better; you'll spend less time feeling depressed, angry, and anxious, giving you more time to enjoy with your friends, lovers, and family. You'll do more with your life, setting and reaching goals to gain a greater sense of contentment.

You'll learn to help yourself with a proven, evidence-based, self-help method that emphasizes the use of your own reasoning power to achieve personal control and growth. You'll learn to look at yourself and others with greater understanding. You'll develop wisdom that will astound others. You'll approach life's challenges calmly, courageously, and compassionately.

Happy for Life offers more than mere inspiration. It gives you ten key strategies and techniques to bring about permanent change so your life is more liveable and enjoyable.

* * *

1 CHOOSE THE DIRECTION OF YOUR LIFE

As far as we know, this is the only life you'll ever have. So you'd better make the most of it. You'd better spend your time doing the things you want to do, seeing the things you want to see, going places you want to go, learning the things you want to learn, doing the kind of work you want to do, and spending time with the people you want to be with.

From now on, decide that you'll lead a goal-oriented life. Set a variety of goals for yourself. Some for your near-term future; some for your mid-term future; and some for your long-term future. Decide what you want to do this week, over the coming months, and over the years ahead. Obviously, if you're wise, you'll avoid setting goals for yourself that will get you killed or locked up.

Set a variety of goals. Set goals to help you to keep up with essential tasks at work and at home. Have another set of goals to help you gain both pleasure and achievement from your activities. Also have goals to help you avoid unnecessary stress while fostering good relationships with others. Remember to set goals to help you enjoy life — don't just focus on work-related goals. Life isn't an examination to prove how good you are — it's an opportunity to enjoy yourself.

Once you've set yourself a series of goals, make them happen. Commit yourself to doing what needs to be done to lead the kind of life you want to lead. Keep checking your progress to see how you're doing. Make sure that in the pursuit of your short-term goals, you don't neglect your long-term goals.

From time to time, revise your goals. As your circumstances change, you may decide that some goals are no longer desirable and that other ones have replaced them. Be willing to amend your goal list whenever necessary.

If life seems dull and boring and you find you've got yourself into a rut, do all you can to get yourself out of it. Decide what you'd rather be doing, and do what's necessary to follow your dream. Don't allow fear of failure or disapproval to hold you back.

A final word of warning: It's important that you don't turn your goals into commandments that *must* be obeyed. If you *insist* on reaching your goals, without allowing yourself to fail, they'll become millstones around your neck. They'll drag you down and hold you back. If you're giving yourself a hard time for not reaching your goals, they're no longer goals. They've become demands. They're toxic and are no longer your friend. You're better off without them.

It's much better for you to think of your goals as rewards — rewards you choose to give yourself simply for being alive.

* * *

2 SEPARATE UNHELPFUL FEELINGS FROM HELPFUL FEELINGS

There's no reason why your life should be easy. From time to time, hopefully not too often, you'll run into difficulties and challenges, and you'll run into obstacles that block you from your goals. When this happens, don't expect to be happy. You'll probably feel bad — that's normal. Bad feelings are an inevitable part of life.

But some feelings are worse than others. Some are healthy and helpful, while others are unhealthy and unhelpful.

Healthy, helpful negative emotions, such as sadness and annoyance, may feel unpleasant, but they don't last forever and they'll often motivate you to make changes in your life — changes that will help you to reach your goals.

On the other hand, unhealthy, unhelpful negative emotions, such as depression, anxiety, and rage are more extreme — they make you feel far worse than you need to. They tend to hang around long after the event; they interfere with other areas of your life; and they make it harder for you to make the changes necessary to reach your goals.

As if that weren't bad enough, you sometimes experience unhelpful feelings about unhelpful feelings. For example, you feel ashamed for having a temper tantrum, you feel afraid of anxiety and panic, and you feel depressed about being depressed.

The good news is that you have the power to change unhealthy, unhelpful negative emotions into their more helpful alternatives. And as long as you choose to exercise that power, you rarely need to suffer from unhealthy, unhelpful negative emotions.

You experience unhelpful emotions when you demand that things be different from the way they are. Instead of merely wishing or wanting things to be different, you insist on it, you demand it, you command it. At first, you may not realize that you're making demands. You may even try to deny that you're doing anything of the sort. But if you pay careful attention to your inner dialogue, and are completely honest with yourself, you'll soon see that's exactly what you're doing.

In other words, you — yes, you! — create your own unhelpful feelings. But because you create them, you can uncreate them. The way to rid yourself of unhelpful, unhealthy negative feelings is to stubbornly refuse to demand changes in your life, to stubbornly refuse to insist that things be different, to stubbornly refuse to command yourself, others, or life in general to submit to your wishes.

By all means, do what you can to improve things. Hang on to your desires and goals. Cherish and pursue them with all the vigor you can muster. But don't make the mistake of demanding that you get what you want or of demanding that you avoid what you don't want.

When you stop making demands on yourself, on others, and life in general, you'll feel better immediately. But feeling better isn't enough. Make it your goal to stay better. Make it your goal to seldom experience unhealthy, unhelpful, negative emotions. With practice, you can enjoy a life where you rarely experience unhelpful emotions, and on the odd occasion when you do experience them, they are not as intense, and they disappear rapidly.

Without interference from unhealthy, unhelpful negative emotions, you can experience the life of your dreams.

* * *

3 RECOGNIZE THE THREE MAJOR DEMANDS

You're not alone. Every one of us has the tendency to turn our desires and preferences into demands. It's part of our evolutionary make up. In the distant past, our ancestors' insistences kept them safe and alive. But in these modern times, we don't need to insist on getting what we want. We can survive quite nicely, thank you very much, by pursuing our preferences and goals without turning them into demands.

The problems and challenges you face don't make you upset: you make yourself upset with your demands. What kind of demands? Well, basically, there are three major demands:

1. I *must* not make mistakes. I *must* do well and win the approval of others for my performances, otherwise I'm no good.
2. Other people *must* treat me considerately, fairly, and kindly — exactly the way I want them to treat me, otherwise they're rotten people and deserve to be punished.
3. Life *must* be comfortable and easy. I *must* get what I want, when I want it. And I *must* not get what I don't want. When things are not the way they *should* be, it's awful and I can't stand it.

Each time you make a demand on yourself, other people, or life in general, you'll also evaluate yourself, others, and the world in extreme and over-generalized ways. Instead of seeing a situation as merely bad or inconvenient, you'll tell yourself that it's *awful* — practically the end of the world. Instead of reassuring yourself that you can survive the situation, you'll convince yourself you *can't stand it*. And you'll tell yourself that the people responsible for the situation — including yourself — are *subhuman* and *damnable*.

These demands are with you all the time. Every time you get upset or behave in self-defeating ways, it's because — knowingly or unknowingly — you're making one or more of these irrational demands. As we've already seen, the tendency to make these kinds of demands is part of the human condition. You can never entirely eliminate the tendency. Even if you can stop making one kind of demand, other demands will replace it. So it's important to be vigilant, to be on your guard against demands, and to destroy them the moment you see them.

Now you have an advantage. You know the harm that demands can do to you. This puts you ahead of the pack. You're now in the fortunate position where you can reduce your demands and correspondingly increase your happiness and contentment in life. The question is: Will you?

* * *

4 REPLACE YOUR DEMANDS WITH PREFERENCES

If you consistently replace your demands with preferences, it's almost impossible to remain upset for any length of time. But how do you replace demands with preferences?

The number one key to an ethical, rewarding, and joyous life is to think like a scientist. Regard your demands as hypotheses to be tested — not as facts. Use scientific enquiry to show that your demands are self-defeating, illogical, and non-factual. You can use scientific analysis to avoid holding inflexible, dogmatic beliefs about yourself, others, and the world in general.

Unhealthy, unhelpful, negative emotions alert you to the fact that you're making a demand. Use these feelings as a reminder to look for the demand that's creating them. Once you've found the demand, ask yourself the following three key questions:

1. Over the long run, does it help me or harm me to demand this? If it harms me, what thought would help me reach my goals better? What thought would make me feel better?
2. Is my demand consistent with the facts? If not, what is consistent with the facts?

3. Does my demand make logical sense? If not, what would make logical sense?

Suppose you're giving yourself a hard time over a mistake you made at work. You tell yourself, "I *shouldn't* have done that. I *should* know better. I'm such an idiot." Notice how your self-condemnation includes demands — demands about what you *should* have done and what you *shouldn't* have done. Now ask yourself the three key questions.

1. Over the long run, does it help you or harm you to make this demand? Obviously it doesn't help you. It doesn't undo the mistake. All it does is make you feel bad. What thought would make you feel better? Answer: "I don't *have* to be perfect. It's unfortunate that I made the mistake, but there's no reason why I *shouldn't* have made it. It's hardly the end of the world. Perhaps with a little time I can repair the damage, learn from the mistake, and try to avoid repeating it in the future."
2. Is your demand consistent with the facts? No it's not. There's no law that says you *must* not make mistakes. In fact, because you're human, you'll frequently make mistakes. Human beings are mistake-making machines. It's what we do. We make mistakes. Every day.
3. Does your demand make logical sense? The fact that you would like to avoid making mistakes doesn't mean you *must* avoid making them. It's a logical fallacy — a *non sequitur* — to go from your desire to avoid making mistakes to the demand that you avoid making them.

Get into the daily habit of questioning your demands. The more you practice questioning your demands, the less frequently you'll succumb to them, and the more rewarding your life will be.

* * *

5 USE THE ABC MODEL

You'll find it easier to question your demands if you use the ABC model created by Dr Albert Ellis. Here's how it works:

A. Something happens.

B. You make a demand about the situation.

C. You have an emotional reaction to the demand.

Here's an example that shows the ABC model in action.

Something happens, (for example, your best friend lies to you) and you react (for example, you get angry). Remember that being lied to doesn't cause the anger. It's your demands about being lied to that make you angry. In simple, ABC terms we have the following:

A. Something happens (in this case, being lied to)

B. Belief or demand (about the lie)

C. Reaction as a result of the demand (anger)

It looks like this:

A. My best friend lied to me.

B. She *shouldn't* lie to me. She *must* always tell me the truth.

C. I feel angry.

Here's another example that shows how changing your beliefs changes your feelings:

A. I have to give a speech at work.

B. I *mustn't* make a fool of myself by giving a poor speech.

C. I feel anxious.

If you had made a different demand, your emotional response would have been different:

A. I have to give a speech at work.

B. I *shouldn't* have to give a speech. I can't stand being told what to do.

C. I feel resentful and angry.

The ABC model shows that **A** (what happens) does not cause **C** (your feelings). It's **B** (your demands) that cause **C**. It's not your friend's lie that made you angry; it's your demand that your friend *shouldn't* have lied to you and *must* always tell the truth. It's not having to give a speech that makes you feel anxious; it's the demand that you *mustn't* make a fool of yourself by giving a poor speech.

Remember: You can't feel angry unless you demand that something or somebody *must* act differently from the way they have been acting; you can't feel anxious unless you believe that you *must* avoid an unpleasant or difficult situation; and you can't feel depressed unless you believe that you *must* be better than you are or life *must* be better than it is.

Once you've found your irrational demands, dispute them vigorously and relentlessly until you no longer believe them. Ask yourself the three key questions:

1. Over the long run, does it help me or harm me to demand this? If it harms me, what thought would help me reach my goals better? What thought would make me feel better?
2. Is my demand consistent with the facts? If not, what is consistent with the facts?
3. Does my demand make logical sense? If not, what would make logical sense?

You can dispute your demands and other irrational beliefs when you're upset. But you can also dispute them when you're not upset. The more often you practice disputing your demands and other irrational beliefs, the less frequently and the less intensely you'll feel depressed, anxious, or angry. And the less often you experience these debilitating emotions, the more time you'll be able to devote to enjoying your life and making the most of it.

* * *

6 CREATE A RATIONAL COPING STATEMENT

Once you've disputed your demands and other irrational beliefs, you can create a rational coping statement and say it to yourself over and over. A rational coping statement has three parts:

1. An acknowledgement of what you want or don't want.
2. The conjunction "but."
3. A contradiction of the demand.

Here are some examples:

- I want to give a good speech but I don't *have* to do so.
- I wish my friend had told me the truth but there's no reason why she absolutely *must* tell me the truth.
- I don't like being told what to do but there's no reason why others — especially my employers — *mustn't* tell me what to do.

An effective rational coping statement is always expressed in the same order. If you change the order of the rational coping statement, you'll find it's not as strong or as effective at rejecting the demand. For example, "I don't *have* to give a good speech but I want to" won't help you overcome your anxiety as much as "I want to give a good speech but I don't *have* to."

Once you've created a three-part rational coping statement, repeat it to yourself over and over. Don't merely parrot the statement, but think about it carefully. Think about how it applies to actual situations in your life. Keep thinking about it and repeating it until you genuinely believe it.

Don't settle for having a so-so belief in the new, rational philosophy behind the coping statement. You don't *have* to get what you want; you don't *have* to get your own way. You don't *have* to do everything perfectly and win the approval of others. Other people don't *have* to do what you want. Life doesn't *have* to give you what you want. Keep working at it until you're thoroughly convinced of it. Use strong language — don't be afraid to throw in the odd expletive or two — emphasizing each word as you repeat it. Do all you can to internalize the effective new philosophy.

Remind yourself — and apply — the three insights of Rational Emotive Behavior Therapy (REBT):

1. Unhelpful emotions such as anger, depression, and anxiety come from demands.
2. You remain anxious, angry, and depressed because you repeat your demands either knowingly — often out loud — or unknowingly.
3. By spending a few minutes every day to reject and rebut your demands you'll experience fewer unhelpful emotions and have more time and energy to enjoy your life.

* * *

7 PRACTICE USING REBT REGULARLY

You'll get more out of life if you make REBT a habit. In his book, *Three Minute Therapy*, my friend and colleague, Dr Michael Edelstein, points out that demands are similar to the buildup of plaque on your teeth. Just as it's necessary to brush your teeth every day to get rid of the plaque, so is it necessary to dispute your demands regularly — daily or even several times a day — to prevent them from interfering with your enjoyment of life.

Here are seven suggestions to help you make REBT a habit:

1. One of the most effective ways to learn a new skill — including and especially REBT — is to teach it to others. Teach REBT to your friends and family. The more you're able to help them, the better you'll understand the principles yourself and how to use them.
2. When you see people acting self-defeatingly, try to figure out what they're telling themselves — what they're demanding — and how they could dispute their demands and other irrational beliefs. It's up to you whether or not you share your observations with these other people.
3. Get to know other people interested in REBT. See if there's an REBT Meetup group in your area, or join an online community of REBT practitioners (for example, https://groups.yahoo.com/group/REBT-CBT-FORUM/).

4. Make recordings of your rational coping statements and play them to yourself regularly. As you listen to them, think about the meaning and try to construct other ways of saying the same thing.
5. Keep reading REBT-based books to remind yourself of the main ideas and philosophies. Naturally, I recommend my own book, *A Guide to Shameless Happiness*, the aforementioned *Three Minute Therapy* as well as books by Dr Ellis, especially *A Guide to Rational Living* and *How to Stubbornly Refuse to Make Yourself Miserable about Anything — Yes, Anything!*
6. Practice rational emotive imagery. Here's how: Imagine yourself in a difficult situation. At first, allow yourself to feel an unhealthy, unhelpful emotion. Then, without changing the situation, ponder a rational coping statement about the situation. For example, imagine people looking down on you as you give a poor speech at work. Allow yourself to feel anxious and stressed. Then, as you continue to see your work colleagues looking down on you, think to yourself, "I would've liked to have given a better speech but there's no reason why I must be a perfect public speaker; it's okay to be a fallible human being — just like everyone else. I'd like the approval of my colleagues but I don't need it." Dwell on this thought, and others just like it, until you no longer feel stressed and anxious despite your colleagues' disapproval.
7. In the final years of his life, Dr Ellis promoted his work through the REBT Network and its website (http://www.rebtnetwork.org/). If you visit the website, you can learn more about REBT and use online forms to help you dispute and change your demands and other irrational beliefs.

* * *

8 BE READY WHEN YOU REVERT BACK TO OLD HABITS

As with any new habit, it's normal to have setbacks. The same is true with getting into the habit of using REBT to improve the quality of your life. When you're faced with a difficult or unpleasant situation, don't be surprised if you forget to use the strategies and techniques you've learned in this book. Backsliding is something that happens to most people — even after they've seen unparalleled improvement in the quality of their lives and in their emotional well-being.

A relapse is nothing to be ashamed of. A relapse doesn't prove you're weak or defective. In an ideal world, you'd practice REBT regularly but there's no law of the universe that says you *must* be perfect at REBT. Forgetting to use the strategies and techniques doesn't make you subhuman — in fact, it proves that you're fully human. Like everyone else on the planet, you're a fallible human being. Welcome to the club. Don't let anyone ever take away your right to be imperfect. And especially, don't take it away yourself.

Instead of putting yourself down, acknowledge your forgetfulness, then get back to work. Eradicating your demands takes work and practice. Work and practice. Work and practice. Look for your *shoulds*; look for your *musts*. Once you've found them, kick the living daylights out of them. They're all that stands between you, your goals, and your happiness. They're your enemy. Treat them as such.

Use the ABC model to find the demand and overcome your self-downing:

A. I forgot to use REBT during a difficult situation and made myself anxious instead of calm.

B. I *must* always remember to use REBT. I'm such an idiot.

C. I feel angry with myself.

When you use REBT strategies and techniques, you can see the situation more calmly, courageously, and compassionately. When you challenge and dispute your demands, you quickly see there's no law of the universe that says you *must* always remember to use REBT. Forgetting to use REBT doesn't make you an idiot. It merely proves that you're sometimes forgetful — a very human trait. Putting yourself down won't help you remember to use REBT in the future. All it does is make you feel angry with yourself — a complete waste of time and energy that could be better spent pursuing your goals.

I'm a strong advocate of teaching yourself to use REBT and practice it regularly. But if you have trouble with it, consult a psychologist, life coach, or psychotherapist who practices REBT and have him or her reinforce and encourage the techniques.

* * *

9 REACH OUT OF YOUR COMFORT ZONE

To reach all your goals, it may be necessary, from time to time, for you to go outside your comfort zone — to do things you're afraid of doing. This is especially true if you cling to the first of the three major demands: I *must* not make mistakes. I *must* do well and win the approval of others for my performances, otherwise I'm no good.

But you can dispute and challenge this demand. You can remind yourself: "I prefer not to make mistakes but there's no reason why I *mustn't* make them. Similarly, I prefer to do well and to win the approval of others but I don't *have* to. Making mistakes and having inadequacies merely proves that I'm human. If I want to reach my goal, the best thing for me to do is to give it my best shot. If I succeed — great. If I fail — too bad. I can always try again. If others look down on me for my lack of success, that's their problem — not mine."

Or perhaps you're held back by the third of the three major demands: Life *must* be comfortable and easy. I *must* get what I want, when I want it. And I *must* not get what I don't want. When things are not the way they *should* be, it's awful and I can't stand it.

Again, you can dispute and challenge this demand: "I wish life were comfortable and easy and that my goals could be easily attained but it doesn't *have* to be that way. There's no law that says I *must* get what I want nor one that says I *mustn't* get what I don't want. The sooner I wake up to the natural reality that some of my goals are difficult to achieve, the sooner I can get to work pursuing them. There's no gain without pain. If I put in the effort now, I can enjoy the rewards later. If the goal's worth reaching, then it's worth my while to put in the time and energy to temporarily live with the discomfort and overcome the obstacles."

There's nothing to be achieved by procrastinating. The sooner you face up to unpleasant tasks, the sooner you'll be rid of them. The longer you put off doing the chore, the longer you have to worry about it and make yourself miserable over it. Once it's done, it's done — you can sit back and relax and enjoy the fruits of your labor.

If you wish, you can give yourself an added incentive to get unpleasant, uncomfortable, inconvenient chores out of the way. Set yourself a deadline to complete the task. If you complete the task before the deadline, give yourself a reward. If, on the other hand, you procrastinate and miss the deadline, penalize yourself. For example, if you meet the deadline you could watch a movie or read a book. If you miss the deadline, you can send a donation to a political candidate you despise.

Remember: Your goal is to enjoy life. Throughout the journey to an ethical, rewarding, and joyful life, it's inevitable you'll run into obstacles and challenges. Ignoring them seldom makes them go away. The sooner you overcome those obstacles and challenges, the longer you can spend celebrating and enjoying your life. Go for it!

* * *

10 CHOOSE TO BE RATIONAL

Throughout this book, I've repeated the idea that gaining proficiency in enjoying your life — by replacing your demands with preferences — takes work and practice. I don't want you to be discouraged by this idea. I'd like you to look on your self-improvement and your pursuit of an ethical, rewarding, and joyful life, as an absorbing challenge or adventure.

Make staying reasonably happy into a game — a game you're determined to master. You can choose to be happy, and you can choose to throw yourself into the task of making yourself happy with gusto.

Look for and pursue activities you enjoy and find absorbing, interesting, or rewarding. Unless something urgent crops up, put everything else on the backburner and focus on your goals. Try to spend as much time as you can participating in these activities.

Above all, remember these important ideas:

1. You don't *need* love and approval and you don't *have* to avoid disapproval.
2. You don't *have* to achieve or succeed at everything you do, and you don't *have* to avoid mistakes.

3. People — including you and those closest to you — don't *have* to do the right thing. Blaming and condemning people for their mistakes will not make them better people.
4. There's no law that says things *must* be the way you want them to be; you *can stand* disappointment.
5. Unhelpful emotions are not caused by circumstances; they are caused by your *demands*.
6. Worrying about dangerous, unpleasant, or frightening events won't prevent them from happening.
7. Avoiding life's difficulties and challenges won't make you happier; the sooner you deal with them the better.
8. It's okay to seek help on the odd occasion when it's useful, but most of the time you don't need someone stronger than yourself to rely on.
9. Events in your past don't cause your unhelpful emotions; your unhelpful emotions come from the *demands* you have about your past, your present, and your future.
10. You don't *have* to feel upset when other people have problems, and you don't *have* to feel unhappy when they're sad.
11. You're not exempt from life's challenges; there's no reason why you *shouldn't* feel discomfort and pain in pursuit of your goals.
12. Most problems have a number of solutions — some better than others; there's no reason why you *must* find a perfect solution to your problems.

Choose to be happy for life. Make it your number one goal to thoroughly enjoy yourself. Have a ball. Today and tomorrow. That's why you're here.

* * *

ABOUT THE AUTHOR

Will Ross taught himself how to use Rational Emotive Behavior Therapy (REBT) and now teaches other REBT self-helpers. He is the author and publisher of online REBT self-help materials and the co-founder of the REBT Network, a major online resource for REBT practitioners, their clients, and students of REBT. This is how he describes his work:

"When Albert Ellis created Rational Emotive Behavior Therapy in the 1950's, he created one of the first self-help therapies. Many people can teach themselves REBT as I did, but some people need extra help. That's what I do: I tutor people who want extra help. Over the years, I've created a number of self-help tools and written a number of articles designed to help people help themselves with REBT. I also work privately, one-on-one, with those who request it, helping them to remain focused and master the techniques and philosophy so that they can overcome their problems, reach their goals, and lead a rewarding and joyous life."

AUTHOR'S NOTE

This book is designed to provide accurate information in regard to the subject matter covered. It is distributed with the understanding that it is not a substitute for psychological, medical, or other professional services. If expert assistance or counseling is needed, the services of a competent professional should be sought.

Please help spread the word.

If you enjoyed this book and found it helpful, please leave a review at Amazon. Your review will encourage others to discover the benefits of REBT.

Gratefully,

Will Ross

Printed in Great Britain
by Amazon